P9-DUB-686

Rimbaud

VERSIONS & INVENTIONS

...still unilluminated I...

WITHDRAWN
UTSA LIBRARIES

ALSO BY STEPHEN BERG

POETRY AND PROSE POETRY

Bearing Weapons
The Queen's Triangle
The Daughters
Nothing in the Word: Versions of Aztec songs
Clouded Sky by Miklos Radnoti (with Steven Polgar and S. J. Marks)
Grief: Poems & Versions of Poems
Oedipus The King (with Diskin Clay)
With Akhmatova at the Black Gates
Sea Ice: Versions of Eskimo Songs
In It
Home to the afterlife
Crow with No Mouth: Ikkyū
New & Selected Poems
Sleeping Woman (public art project with the painter Tom Chimes)
The Steel Cricket: Versions 1958-1997
Oblivion
Shaving
Porno Diva Numero Uno
Halo
Footnotes to an Unfinished Poem
X=
The Elegy on Hats

ANTHOLOGIES

Naked Poetry (with Robert Mezey)
Between People (with S. J. Marks and J. Michael Pilz)
About Women (with S. J. Marks)
In Praise of What Persists
Singular Voices
The Body Electric (with David Bonanno & Arthur Vogelsang)
My Business is Circumference

Rimbaud
VERSIONS & INVENTIONS

...still unilluminated I...

STEPHEN BERG

THE SHEEP MEADOW PRESS
RIVERDALE-ON-HUDSON, NEW YORK

Library
University of Texas
at San Antonio

Copyright © 2005 by Stephen Berg.

All rights reserved. No part of this publication may be reproduced or transmitted in any form or by any means, electronic or mechanical, including photocopying, recording, or any information storage and retrieval system, without the express written consent of the publisher.

All inquiries and permission requests should be addressed to:
The Sheep Meadow Press, P.O. Box 1345
Riverdale-on-Hudson, NY 10471

Design: Eileen Neff
Typeset by The Sheep Meadow Press.
Distributed by The University Press of New England.

Printed on acid-free paper in the United States. This book meets the guidelines for permanence and durability of the Committee on Production Guidelines for Book Longevity of the Council on Library Resources.

The Library of Congress Cataloging-in-Publication Data
Berg, Stephen.
 Rimbaud versions & inventions : still unilluminated i / Stephen Berg
     p. cm.
 ISBN 1-931357-96-X (pbk. : alk. paper)
1. Rimbaud, Arthur, 1854-1891--Adaptations. 2. Rimbaud, Arthur, 1854-1891--Parodies, imitations, etc. I. Title: Rimbaud versions and inventions. II. Title.

PS3552.E7R56 2005
811'.54--dc22

2005003354

Special thanks to The Daniel W. Dietrich Foundation for a grant that made possible the design of this book.

Library
University of Texas
at San Antonio

Part IV of this book, the series of prose poems called "Rimbaud," first appeared in the book *Oblivion*.

Some of the sonnets in Part I use phrases of Rimbaud's for titles, while the poems themselves are mine.

My thanks to Len Roberts for his many valuable suggestions for revision while the book was being written

TABLE OF CONTENTS

I

Evening Prayer / 3
My Bohemian Life / 4
At the Green Inn / 5
Venus / 6
The Flirt / 7
"...Wept More than all the Children in the World" / 8
"...Disappearing and Reappearing..." / 9
"...Peacefully, Opening my Nostrils..." / 10
"I See my Spirit is Sleeping" / 11
"Why Golden Stars Swarming like Sand?" / 12
"I Do Not Say a Word: I..." / 13
"...The Extent of my Innocence..." / 14
"...Still Unilluminated..." / 15
"...Agate, Mahogany, Gold..." / 16

II

Sealed Lips / 18
Young GreedyGuts / 19
Eternity / 20
Pleasant Thoughts: Morning / 21
The Highest Tower / 22
Romance / 23
Musical Scene / 25
Crows / 27
Young Couple / 28
Cursed Angel / 29
Winter Dream / 30
Shame / 31
Cheated Heart / 32
Tear / 33

Evil / 34
Verses by Dr. Coppee / 35
Dance of the Hanged Men / 38
Transfixed / 40
Sisters of Charity / 42
The Poor in Church / 44
Old Men Sitting / 46
First Twilight / 48
Defilements / 50
My Little Lovers / 51
Memories of a Simple-Minded Old Man / 53
May Banners / 55

III

Chair: Fragments / 58
Lice Killers / 60
Parisian Orgy / 61
Her Hands / 64
Sleeper in the Valley / 66
Blackcurrant River / 67
Faun's Head / 68
Lilies / 69
Cupboard / 70
Paroxysms of Caesars / 71
Ophelia / 72
Thirst: Fragments / 74
Squatting / 75
The Just Man / 77
Feasts of Hunger / 79
Last Lines: Memory: God / 80

RIMBAUD
IV

The Impossible / 84
Lightning / 86
Happiness / 87
Words / 88
Blacks / 89
Image / 90
God / 91
Pain / 92
Sublimity / 93
Hands / 94
Seeds / 95
Nostalgia / 96
Impasse Metanoia / 97
Angel / 98
Dawn / 99
Beauty / 100

Afterword / 101

"The poet would define the amount of the unknown awakening in the universal soul in his own time. . . ."
—Rimbaud, Letter to Paul Demeny, Charleville, 15 May 1871

"...STILL UNILLUMINATED I..."

I

EVENING PRAYER

I live seated in a barber's chair, wild angel
getting a haircut, I hold a fluted mug,
neck bent, belly stuck out, biting a clay pipe.
Swollen impalpable veils of smoke blind me.
Ten million dreams smolder in my brain
like warm excrement coating a pigeonhouse floor.
Sometimes my gnarled heart is a sapling
each inch beaded with young brown-gold blood,
but I shyly swallow my dreams, guzzle
thirty or forty mugs—a boy taking communion—
then stand at attention to relieve the bitter need:
King of cedar and hyssops, with the consent
of the lush purplish heliotropes, I sweetly piss
very high, very far, aiming at the furious skies.

MY BOHEMIAN LIFE

I jammed my fists into my torn pockets and took off,
my coat was beginning to look just right,
a big hole near my ass in my one pair of pants shone like a coin.
Muse, I was your slave, I wore the sky like a crown.
A dazed midget, I slept in the Big Dipper,
blew endless rhymes on the wind as I went.
What amazing torch-like loves scorched my dreams!
My own stars spoke to me like softly clashing reeds—
I listened to them sitting on the grassy
roadside stones those cool September nights
when dew graced my forehead like a strong Burgundy,
I wrote among unreal shadows, an unreal shadow
myself, and plucked the black elastics of my
wounded shoes like a lyre, one foot pulled up against my heart!

AT THE GREEN INN

For a week on the road stones slashed my boots.
I reached Charleroi. At the Cabaret-Vert
I ordered bread and butter, half-chilled ham,
stretched my legs under the green table happily,
studied the wallpaper's corny
washed-out roses—what a succulent piece
with huge tits and euphoric eyes served me
the bread and butter, warm ham on a plate
incised with oak leaves, giggling as she leaned
close to my face, one garlic clove sticking
out of the rosy meat, her mouth nothing
but a slit while she filled my giant mug,
pink tongue visible between guileless lips,
late sunlight gilding the abundant foam!

VENUS

Brown hair gleaming with pomade,
bald spots showing through dabs of powder,
thick greasy neck, wide shoulder-blades protruding,
concave stump of a back bulging—a woman
totters up from an old green zinc
coffin of a bathtub.
The globes of the buttocks seem to veer off,
fat slabs slide and ripple under the skin;
spine scabbed with a bloody rash, this thing reeks like a garbage
    pail—
you need a magnifying glass
to see the weird details: ass-cheeks tattooed
        CLARA VENUS
now the entire carcass squirms and displays its massive rump over
    the tub edge,
hideous exquisite anus decorated with an ulcer.

THE FLIRT

Brown dining room, varnish and apples sweeten the air;
I ladle out some Belgian stew into a bowl,
put bread on a plate, sit back in my plush armchair.
The unconscious clock is happy, its pendulum
kicks the bright brass gears as I eat.
The kitchen door flies open, air
gusts from it against my face; through it
a servant girl comes up to me—I'm not sure why—
her neckerchief untied, hair swept up in a bun,
fusses with the nearby plates—to make me cozier?
more relaxed?—checks the peach fuzz skin
of her left cheek with a forefinger, lips
pouting like a three-year-old's, then just like that,
so I'll kiss her, whispers, "Feel here . . . I've caught a cold . . ."

"...WEPT MORE THAN ALL THE CHILDREN IN THE WORLD"

No matter where I was I was you I
ate what you ate sour green apples bread
staler than a dead man's locked mouth rancid
meat of the poor I was the one who could
not help you no matter what I did: to
be you was my hopeless love I saw what
you saw sheets of blood and coal money fixed
high on the blind throne of power
prayer pulverized by the teeth of slaughter
and when I bent to kiss you you weren't there
when I reached for your hand it was plain air
all the children in the world
begging me whispering my lost names no
matter who I was what I could not do

"... DISAPPEARING AND REAPPEARING ..."

In some strange dream where you saw toys I saw
myself thought of by God the way children
are *in* God when they play until someone
interrupts *Dinnertime...wash your hands!*
have you ever forgotten yourself completely
become death become each act word
because sleep existed throughout the day
without you though you were there
in it *of* it *it* without not being you?
this does happen to those whose torment kills
who they were before some dire humbling luck
afflicted fate with the crucifix
of rotted names they were nailed to
in a strange dream in the speechless mind of God

"... PEACEFULLY, OPENING MY NOSTRILS ..."

I was obsessed with shutting myself up
in outhouses scaring the rats away pants
at my ankles book and pencil in hand
reveling in the tepid stench of ripe shit
on all four walls flies waited patiently
to garnish the rising heap again under
the butt-hole this time I read Stendhal's acidic
Henri Brulard underlining sentences
bracketing paragraphs phrases "What then
have I been? I can't know." when I was done
I stayed there judging the fecal wafts—
Did my dump change the mixture:
less pungent eloquence? a bit sweeter?—
counting flies clinging to the door like black tears

"I SEE MY SPIRIT IS SLEEPING"

I live "like a spark of gold of pure light"
no identity no otherness no
name a leaf could easily wreck my soul
as reefs gash a cardboard ship this gold
of my being this light this pure non–
entity of flesh of soul seeing
that's what I mean this spark can't be put out
by the face of the prehistoric pain
I wake to every day where one
muffled voice throbs even when I eat
pray put on shoes incandescent elegy
of hands of the foot in leather of earth
to walk on I live like the warm darkness
between the lining of the shoe and the foot

"WHY GOLDEN STARS SWARMING LIKE SAND?"

Embryos rays of light the face His face
who must have known it would be like this who
became himself more stars then blinding
the entire sky swarming into a halo
not one thorn not one word to explain why
nothing will ever explain this
nobody will ever touch His quiet face now
the white swarm of indistinct dreams questions
hissing around the eyes red pigeons hymns
the mind a city of dead citizens
lice eternity like a baby's fist
no resurrection no death no holy man
my heart and my flesh kissed by His flesh
seethe with the putrefied kiss of Jesus

"I DO NOT SAY A WORD: I . . ."

keep looking at the skin of their white necks
embroidered with stray locks I reconstruct
their bodies wracked flayed with fever quaking
like insects champagne can cannot stop me
an orphan mothered by angels I study
their mammoth wings I let them kiss my face feet
like electric butterflies green dioptrics
all I am is essence matter Goodbye
all I want is the nothingness of all
things not to be as objects are
this is for the man who has seen enough
this is for the man who has known enough
why isn't a flower a man with human blood
why isn't stone a man with human blood

"...THE EXTENT OF MY INNOCENCE..."

Nothing's left of me not even the weight
of experience like a red wall against
the sky now I know prayer is the only
present tense for the soul not to need words
not to need silence prayer's anything seen
heard touched now I can rest seeing
the civilized killer I was how cash
was poetry getting sucked off firing
a pistol into a friend's arm smoking dope
doors to those sacred time-sparks without God
here for the first time I can't feel the wool
of my shirt my beret my socks knees
I bite my silk scarf topped with violet fog
identity's infinite Now where I am

". . . STILL UNILLUMINATED . . ."

I die leaping through nameless unheard of things
fearless pitiful beauty pimps thieves saints
rich women wet with passion and silk
whose list should it be the man I was am
will be? plum tree cobalt fork sink broom stacks
of hundred dollar bills in my last bedroom
bowls swollen with the cold white diamonds of pain
what erased hatred completely was your mouth
how could I have known before it covered mine
what made grief impossible were your hands
how could I have known until you touched me
what transfigured immortality into actual flesh
were the words you spoke one night leaning over me
galactic signs a billion light years away

"...AGATE, MAHOGANY, GOLD ..."

It's over nothing but things now nothing but
qualities the I the We the You gone
nobody to watch clouds tatter and flee
blue scraps evaporating nobody to feed
finches sparrows wrens so vulnerable
crowding the feeder hung on the birch branch
unseen stars unseen rivers unseen rocks
now this life means the Real unseen
not one human eye left to base
calculations on whether green oval
oblong thin cold square no human breath
to mist the empty mirrors who
speaks these words never was now only
otherness truth in one soul one body

II

SEALED LIPS

Rome, in the Sistine Chapel
encrusted with symbols of Christ—
a petite scarlet skullcap
filled with antique shriveling noses:

Thebaid ascetics' noses,
noses of canons of the Holy Grail,
nostrils packed with coagulated lead-gray night
and the drone of funereal plainsong.

Each morning into their mystic
desiccated kingdom schismatic
waste crushed to a fine powder
is carefully poured.

YOUNG GREEDYGUTS

Wrinkled silk
cap,
ivory
penis,

black
shirt, jacket, pants,
Paul studies
the cabinet,

sticks his rigid
tongue out
at a ripe pear,
gets ready,

pokes it
with the tip
repeatedly until
juice seeps out.

ETERNITY

I found it again.
What? Eternity:
the sea's run off
with the blazing sun.

Watchman soul,
let's whisper a confession
of night's nothingness
and the fiery day.

From praise, from mankind's
lust, you meet me here,
then fly away
your way, your way.

Only you, satiny
red embers, breathe
Duty, but nobody
cries out "Finally!"

No hope here.
Knowledge, stamina—
-I can't be sure
they'll torture me.

Found again. What?
Eternity: the
sea escaping every-
where with the sun.

PLEASANT THOUGHTS: MORNING

It's morning, summer, four o'clock,
love's still vibrating here. Dawn's musky smells
from last night float under the spinnakers;

trapped in the vast workshop
near the Hesperidean sun
carpenters in rolled-up sleeves are awake

in their wasteland of foam peacefully
stitching posh urban canopies to shade
gold-set leering gems under enamelled skies.

Just for the sake of the workers
Love leaves the lovers alone, souls
laureled with remnants of their juices.

Queen of caretakers, give the destitute men
down there hard liquor to soothe their colossal muscles
until the sea lulls them, bathing at noon.

THE HIGHEST TOWER

My whole youth I was a slave to idleness,
so sensitive I wasted my life. Let the time come

when hearts are in love with love, "Let be," I said
to myself, "let no one see you, give up the promise

of finer joys, let nothing stop your majestic
withdrawal from the world." I've held on so long

I've forgotten everything: anguish is lost
to the skies, sick thirst roves like a shadow in my veins.

That's why the meadow was sacrificed to oblivion,
dense with grasses and flowers, frankincense, tares,

to the elated humming of a hundred filthy flies.
Oh! thousands of griefs the absurd soul

lives on nothing more than the Virgin Mary's image!
Can a human being pray to the Virgin Mary?

Youth was a slave to everything; too sensitive,
I've wasted my life. Let hearts love love, immediately!

ROMANCE

At seventeen you're not really serious.
One fine night you've swilled enough lemonade and beer.
Fed up with the din of garishly-lit cafes,
you walk out admiring the promenade's green lime trees.

The fruit smells fantastic on clear June evenings.
The air's so soft you close your eyes to let your eyelids feel it.
The wind chattering across from the nearby town
is soaked in the perfume of vines and beer.

A flash of miniscule blue-black rag
framed by a skinny branch, pierced by a gloomy
perfectly white fragile pinpoint shivering star
that dissolves into the blackest distance.

Night. June. Seventeen. You let yourself get drunk
on champagne, your head nearly explodes from it.
You wobble down streets, feel a kiss on your lips
like the sting of some tiny insect.

Your fucked-up heart Crusoes through each of your romances—
charming haughty girl spotlighted by a dim streetlamp,
her father's high stiff collar grazes her cheek, terrifies you;
you're ridiculously naïve, she feels, and trots off

in her glossy ankle boots, hearing you sigh.
You're in love, knocked off your feet until August.
Your sonnets make her laugh, your friends disappear,
you're not in style—then this goddess

condescends one evening to write you a letter.
That night you're back in the cafes, for beer,
for lemonade, not really serious at seventeen,
the lime trees in brilliant full leaf along the promenade.

MUSICAL SCENE

Irises planted in rows, trees pampered in moats
of topsoil and mulch, this oasis chopped into nasty
little squares, awash in the lamplight's blush,
is perfect. The wheezy elder citizens, driven

outdoors by the heat, mumble their silly jealousies.
The military band's drums and tinny trumpets
blare from the bandstand over the town dandy,
the notary dangles like a charm from his own watch chain.

Trust funds wearing pince-nez point out all
the false notes; bank desks drag their fat wives
in their wake. On the green iron benches retired
grocers poke the sand with their knobbed walking

sticks, solemn about trade agreements, then pinch
snuff out of silver boxes and begin again:
"In short! . . ." One obese banker spreads his behind
across his bench, pale yellow shiny

buttons dot his vest; a Flemish corporation
smokes his expensive pipe, tobacco shreds
hang from it. Sprawled all along the borders
of the grass bums jeer, simple-minded

foot-soldiers suck roses, fondle the nurses'
babies to seduce the nurses. Like a disheveled student,
under budded chestnuts, I follow the cute
girls—they know I'm there, turn back to me, chuckle,

eyes rabid with salacious things. I say
nothing, focus on the skin of their creamy necks
embellished with curls, search their translucent
blouses, skirts, kiss their celestial backs

just below the curve of the shoulders and soon
stroke stocking and boot. I recreate their bodies
fevered with fantasies of nakedness. They think I'm an idiot,
whisper about me. I want to fuck their mouths.

CROWS

O Lord, when the meadows are frosty
and the Angelus in each drab village
is silent, let the dear rapturous crows
sweep down on this flowerless earth.

Eerie army scattering your shrill bleak cries,
winds batter and freeze your nests!
Over sallow rivers, ditches, holes, roads
clogged with ghost cavalry, disperse,

black allies, blanket the French fields
where the day before yesterday's
dead sleep, wheel over us in winter, please.
All travelers should remember you!

Therefore, inspire men to their work,
sleek emblem of humanity's grief.
Saints of sky, clustered at the top of the oak,
(masthead misted by the inhabited twilight),

leave the singing wrens and finches alone—
in endless woods, in prisons of inexorable
underbrush, slaves of defeat with
no future pace the blameless wilderness.

YOUNG COUPLE

Bluish-green sky floods the room
stacked with boxes and bins, outside
birthwort smothers the wall, elves'

gums tingle, genii decide our fate.
All so expensive, so untidy,
mulberry and hairnets

in the corner put there
by the African fairy.
Several irate godmothers

draped in skirts of light
rummage the cupboards
and hide there. The tenants

are out, they don't care,
nothing gets done.
The bridegroom owns the wind

that cheats him every minute
he's away. Even the mischievous lake
and stream and river sprites

break in and roam among
dusty tables and chairs
and bump dustballs under the bed.

CURSED ANGEL

Night, bluish roofs, white doors, Sundays,
the silent road at the end of the town white,
the street's bizarre windows—shutters made out of angels' wings—
watch him race toward an evil boundary stone that shivers,

black staggering angel gorged on jujubes—
he vomits, vanishes—vile shiny chunks
of his last meal glazed by the stern holy moon,
a shallow cesspool of dirty blood.

WINTER DREAM
To . . . Her

We'll ride in a miniature pink railway car
next winter, stretch out on fat silk cushions
so easy with each other a nest of crazy
kisses waits for us in each corner of the couch.

You'll close your eyes so you can't see night shadows
through the glass make outraged faces, monsters scowl
at you, a whole nation of black devils
and blacker wolves rushing beside the train.

Something tickles your cheek—wild spider
kissing you, circling your neck; vapid indigo hills,
roads, houselights flare on the window

and you bend back your head and say to me
"Find it!" We'll take forever to pluck off that weightless visitor,
that great traveller, crush it or save it in a jewel box.

SHAME

As long as the scalpel hasn't
excised his brain, fatty
graygreen package that spurts
stale steam when the skull is cut—

(really, he should amputate
his nose, lips, ears, belly,
abandon his legs! this most
miraculous, uncanny creature)—

no, I believe that as long
as the blade pressed against his head,
stones piled against his hips, flame
eating his fetid guts

have not executed him,
this boring child, idiotic
as a flounder or monkey,
will always cheat and betray

and, like a Rocky Mountain cat,
stink up the entire planet!
But still, O God, when he dies
let someone mutter a prayer!

CHEATED HEART

My sad heart dribbles at the stern
my heart stained with *caporal* they
squirt jets of soup on it the whole crew
mocks it with a single guffaw

Poor heart covered with *caporal*
lewd ithyphallic erkish their
gibes have smashed it graffiti scrawled
on the wheelhouse ithyphallic dirty words

erkish O abracandic waves
purge my heart take it erkish lewd
ithyphallic blighted by their screams.
When they've finished chewing their tobacco

what shall we do my cheated heart?
Drunk hiccups after they spit out
their mushy plugs then I'll vomit
if I can swallow my heart if

I can figure out why they hate me
these insolent sailors who shout
my name. I stand at the tiller
my heart bleeding through my white shirt.

TEAR

Hundreds of miles from birds and herds and village girls,
I was kneeling in heather fringed by hazel copses;
humid afternoon mist.
What could I have been drinking in that tender place,
no flowers, elms speechless, muddy sky?
What did I fill my gourd with—pale gold cognac
that made me sweat? The way I felt
I should have carved a wooden sign to hang over an inn,
its big gilded letters beckoning.
A storm boiled the sky until evening.
The sign twisted in the wind.
Black nations, lakes, sky-high poles, railway stations.
Pillars, glowing at intervals, measured the blue night.
Water from unidentified peaks trickled into pristine white
      sand.
Wind snarled down icing the ponds.
Like an obsessed fisherman who casts his line for gold, lobster,
      shrimp until sundown
I didn't bother to drink.

EVIL

Grape shot like gobs of red spit whistle all day
through the infinite purple sky; scarlet or pink
battalions near the King who jeers at them
crumble in fire, a hundred thousand men
smashed by insanity, strewn in a smoking heap—
O the pathetic dead! O Nature!—grass
sprouts next to their heads, arms, feet in the joy
you felt shaping these sacred human beings! . . .
God smiles at the damask altar-cloths while
this goes on: He inhales incense, studies
the fat gold chalices, dozes while their inane
lullaby of needy praise floats off like smoke
then wakes when the anxious mothers prostrate
under His eyes, black-bonneted, offer Him
the single penny tied up in their handkerchiefs!

VERSES BY DR. COPPÉE

I

Summer nights trapped in the flaming eyes of the shopfronts
I stand outside vague groups of cheery home-loving people,
suckers on cutty pipes, kissers of strong oily cigars,
I wander into a stone kiosk dark as a closet, imagine Tibet

iced-in by loud clean water, lulling human desire,
hear the vicious north wind that never spares one human vein
    attack—
sap simmers beneath the circular iron grates
radiating above the roots of the lean chestnut trees.

II

In a third-class compartment an old priest stuffs
his briar, sticks his smooth calm forehead out the window
to enjoy the wind, fringe of faded gray hair thrashing,
then this Christian, chaplain once to a royal scion

condemned to death, despite the jokes people might crack,
with sad urgency asks me for a pinch of *caporal*
to ease the boredom of the tunnel coming up, dank black artery
open to travellers at the town of pre-Soissons in Aisne.

No question, in spring I'd rather loaf in that suburban café
under the branches of the May dwarf chestnuts' buds
that swell into leaf near the tidy square. Young dogs,
scolded by their owners, frolic near the Drinkers' statue,

trample the beds of hyacinths bordering it. Until the hyacinths
    bloom,
on the slate table where with a stone in 1720 a deacon
scratched his Latin nickname thin as an inscription on a church
    window,
at night no one gets drunk on the splutter of the black bottles.

III

A miserable bus driver waiting under the shop's tin canopy,
rubbing his gloved frozen hands, watches the heavy
sullen bus he drives during the day thread the left bank,
tears off the purse of carfare he was carrying

against his inflamed groin. Soft shadows thronged with police.
The inside of the bus, empty, respectable, follows the moon
in deep sky rocking among its green cotton-wool clouds;
despite the Edict and the curfew and the fact that the bus

is heading back to L'Odeon, the juvenile hard-ass
keeps screaming incomprehensibly at the unlit town square.

IV

That year when our glorious Prince was born has left me
with such charitably soothing memories of Paris, limpid
as a Swiss lake, where Ns embroidered in gold thread—
snow heaped at the palace gates, on the guillotine

mounting-blocks—cascade like fireworks trailing tricolor ribbon.
In the havoc of crowds, broad sun-bleached hats, waistcoats
festooned with embroidered flowers, old frock-coats, protest songs
shouted over and over by retired workmen in dining-rooms;

at evening, the Emperor, impeccable, boots shiny black, strolls with
the Sainted
Spanish woman stepping on shawls women have laid out every-
where.

The boy who plays ball games, the Pubescent One,
his veins blessed with the blood of exile and a celebrated father,
fantasizing a movie-star face and perfect physique—feels
his existence start to thrive—he hopes to see silk curtains every-
where:

not the throne's, not the crib's; his exquisitely shaped head
and shoulders have no desire to storm the walls of the future!
He has left behind all the worn-out playthings—O his unyielding
dream!
Some naked solitude has made his eyes terribly profound:

Poor young man, unquestionably he's learned how to masturbate!

DANCE OF THE HANGED MEN

Generals are waltzing on puke-black gallows,
one-armed friend, prancing, leaders
skinny as a wristbone, slaves of the devil, skeletons

Beelzebub jerks them up by the scruffs of their necks,
these puppets grinning at the sky, slaps them
across the head backhanded like a kick

making them jig to a corny popular tune—
arms entwined, breasts riddled with light, they
jostle each other in gruesome drawn-out fucks

beauteous gay dancers without bellies or breasts
spinning on heels of bone, they'll never wear out
patent leather pumps, their skin shirts

draped on invisible hooks, no testicles
or cocks, no shame—snow floats onto their skulls
so each one sports a white fluffy hat:

crows serve as plumes for these cracked brains,
goatees of raw flesh drip from their weak chins—
easy to call them stick-like knights

colliding in cardboard armor—Hurray! wind hums
through their bones, the gallows squeal like an iron
pipe organ, from their slimy caves wolves yowl

at the festive music, the sky's a hell-red corpse
a haze along the horizon—these arrogant brain-washed officers
count the women they've loved by fingering each

vertebra like a Catholic telling beads—atheist
ghosts!—one giant of a skeleton breaks away from the dance
leaps into the sky feels the rope tighten again

slams his knuckles against his thigh burbles
like a psychotic about nothing then skips back
into the symphony of bones pelvis to pelvis with a cohort

TRANSFIXED

Kneeling in snow and fog,
shadowy in snow and fog,
butts humped up, five kids stare
at the wide lighted airshaft.

What torture as they watch
the baker knead white
heavy bread, his strong white
arms shaping the gray dough,

setting it in the bright
hole. They hear the good bread
swelling, the baker grins
his pudgy grin, hums a popular tune.

Huddled together, not
one moves, air from the red
vent wafts over them
kind as a mother's breast.

And when, for some midnight
breakfast bread plaited
like a brioche is lifted
out, when under the smoky

beams the fresh sweet crusts hiss
and crickets sing— oh this
oven breathes life itself!
Their souls ravished under

the rags they wear,
life like fire make them so
strong, scrawny frozen Jesuses,
they push their

little pink snouts against
the wire screen, grunting
through the holes, stupidly
mouthing prayers, leaning forward

so hard to feel those lights
of open heaven they split
their pants, their shirt tails
flap in the biting wind.

SISTERS OF CHARITY

The young man with brown skin, criminal
blank eyes, knock-out twenty-year-old body
forced to go naked everywhere, brow
ringed with copper like a Persian prince in moonlight

worshipped by inconceivable spirits; pliable
virginal impulsive soul, proud of his first
willful mistakes, like seas just born, like tears
on summer nights, sleepless on diamond beds,

faced with the world's ugliness, the young man
feels his heart sicken, nothing is good,
his wound's continual unhealing pain
wakens the need for a sister of charity.

But listen, You, cluster of bowels, compassion
sweet as butter—you're never really the Sister
of Charity, never: whorish glance, belly
of chocolate shadow trance, perceptive fingers,

breasts shaped so perfectly one *has* to suck
on them—none of this gives me anything.
Blind unaware slut whose irises rage like cats,
our intimacy is no more than a question

questioning—you are the one who needs *us*,
beast with the breasts—we suckle you, charismatic
mortal Passion. Hate, laziness, inertia, flaws,
torments shouldered for centuries—you whip us

with it all, O night still unmalicious,
with extra blood shed monthly. When Woman
is let in for an instant a man's terrified—love
that makes life possible, hymn that spurs action;

Muse of the green universe and Justice
writhing like a torch, blister his whole body
with their obsessions. Thirsting interminably
for grandeur, peace, forsaken by both crazed

implacable Sisters, whimpering for fact
whose arms will always pull him to her breasts,
he sacrifices his bloodstained head to Nature.
This injured male, this scholar of pride, deems blessed alchemy

and scholarship trash. Nauseating loneliness
marches closer. Then, still irresistible, not appalled
by the coffin, he can only believe in cosmic purposes,
gigantic Dreams or Journeys across the night of truth,

and he must call for you with every cell of his sick limbs and soul.
O mystical death, O deceitful sister of Charity!

THE POOR IN CHURCH

They hunch between oak pews like pigs, lurking
in corners where their sour breath warms the stones;
they ogle the chancel swathed in gold brocade,
watch the twenty choir boys' jaws bawl songs of worship,

inhale the melting wax fumes as if they were fresh bread;
like happy, humble dogs beaten with sticks
they hand their master, God, useless
offerings of cake, fruit, a few paltry coins.

These women love to wear the benches smooth
after the harsh punishment of six days;
they nurse creatures that look like real children
swaddled in frayed shawls, howling as if they'll die.

Their unwashed breasts hang out, their abject eyes
never say a prayer; these soup-eaters
observe a bunch of young delinquents show off
doffing crazily cocked and crushed hats.

Outside is cold and hunger and a man stinking drunk.
Okay, there's one more hour to go, then sicknesses
without names! Meanwhile, wherever you look
old women, wattle-necked, whimper and whisper:

these are the lost people shunned yesterday
at crossings, starved epileptics, crippled girls;
pulled by their dogs to courtyards, shops, the blind
lift crumbling Bibles to their faces as if they see.

And each one drooling mindless degraded faith
with pleading, stiffly gesticulating hands
moans endlessly to Jesus, dreaming up there,
yellow in the window's livid stained glass

high above potbellied businessmen, far
from the stench of meat, starvation, moldy cloth,
and as prayer blossoms in more exquisite words
and mysteries are sung in more emphatic tones

rich women smiling trite green silk smiles walk up and down
the aisles splashed gold by the last fullness of sun—Jesus,
these upperclass ladies with ailing livers!
their long jaundiced fingers kiss holy water in the stoups.

OLD MEN SITTING

Pock marks like hail, gray tumors lumped on their cheeks,
clenched warty feeble hands on their thighs,
eyes grayish rimmed, bald skulls scabrous
with the damp blotchy stains seen on ancient walls—

these humans glue their frail skeletons
to the skeletons of their chairs the way people fucking do,
twist their feet around the rickety rails.
They've always worshipped this benevolent furniture,

flesh wood, wood flesh, sun withering their skin
to calico or else indoors, watching
the window-panes go blind with sleet, they quake
like exhausted toads stuck on an iced-up pond.

Their chairs are kind to them. Straw aged brown
cradles their sore buttocks; they glow inside
as if eons of stars have lived forever there.
The men who sit, knees drawn up to their teeth,

bad pianists, ten fingers drumming the underside
of their seats, listen to each other's bathetic code—
ghost-notes squeezed in-and-out in-and-out
of cracked accordions. Their heads rock back and forth.

It makes you think of the act of love.
Don't force them to get up! It's catastrophic!
They jump hissing like tom-cats slapped away,
enraged, abruptly arching their shoulders.

Their asses swell their pants into small balloons,
they knock the back of their heads hard against
grubby walls, stomping their swollen feet;
at the end of corridors their ebony coat buttons

gleam like chimpanzees' eyes riveted to yours!
They also have an invisible weapon that kills:
stalking you, the quick poison of whipped bitches
seething in their eyes seeps out, you start to sweat

inside a terrifying funnel. They sit down again,
fists retreating into their filthy cuffs.
All they can think of is the idiots who
made them get up. All day their tonsils shudder,

diminutive inward chins ready to burst.
Their lids close, they doze off, heads on their arms,
death-nibblers dreaming of sunburnt nubile lovers
and filigreed open-work chairs at executives' desks.

Ink-blossoms drop pollen like commas punctuating their fate
and rock these souls to sleep; squat flower cups protect their souls;
dragonflies dart through the irises; *membra virilia*
get horny rubbing up against barbed stalks of wheat.

FIRST TWILIGHT

Huge indiscreet cunning trees
clawed the windowpanes,
pressed close—
she wore almost nothing

perched in my fat armchair,
hands folded on her petticoat.
Exquisite feet
didn't touch the floor,

one wand of waxy light
crisscrossed
ecstatic lips, a fly
landed on a rosebud nipple,

a circle of faint clear trills
like a shocked crystal chandelier
broke from her mouth
when I licked her ankles

and both my hands
chased wild feet
through layers of white lace—"No!"
she giggled, clenching her thighs.

Oh those blank animal eyes—
I grazed each lid
with wet lips.
"Too much!" Her head shot back.

"I want to tell you . . ."
I completed her sentence with my tongue
which made her laugh again,
mercifully this time, ready . . . .

Huge indiscreet cunning trees
clawed the windowpanes,
pressed close—
she wore almost nothing.

DEFILEMENTS

Ancient animals fucked running
glans filmed with excremental blood
our fathers showed their cocks
unsheathed them pulled the scrotum up to display it
you needed a huge one to fuck women or pigs
don't envy a rhino's we're big enough

but sadly we've given up wielding our shlongs in public
showing off like children frolicking in the woods
often I've watched men
shitting behind hedges
learned what the ass is for
white skin screened by hair

women have a tuft of it right there
focused like a dark flame
I'd give anything to be naked studying it
I also dreamt of eating the pink reticulated lips that pout
after fucking doused with my sperm
dreamt my mouth was often
open on it
as if proof of a soul depended on that act
as if that *were* my soul
kneeling sucking on it weeping

MY LITTLE LOVERS

Something like human tears
soaks the cabbage-leaf sky,
trees drool,
your raincoats laid out
white with unique moons
like stunned saucer eyes
beneath branches.
Hideous children,
slam your kneecaps together
until they ache.
Blue ugly one,
we were in love then,
we gobbled soft-boiled eggs
and chickweed! Blond ugly one,
one night you gave me the holy name of "poet."
Drape yourself on my lap
so I can lift your skirt and whip you.
Black ugly one,
redheaded ugly one,
I vomited your brilliantine.
O my petite amours,
I hate you,
I'd love to see your tits plastered
with sores, all my sentiments
like smashed mossy old flowerpots.
Jump up, dance for me,
a star pinned to your limping backs,
flex those gaunt shoulder blades
that inspired me to rhyme.
I'll break your hips
for loving me, for getting me hard.
Sweet ugly ones, depraved ugly ones,
mound of dull stars, failed, fallen

through the abyss of God's absence,
my dried saliva glistens on your brow.

MEMORIES OF A SIMPLE-MINDED OLD MAN

If there's a God, forgive me!

As a boy, at country fairs, I avoided
the idiotic shooting gallery's metal ducks, pushovers,
clones gliding across cartoon water under a rigid sky;
I stood awestruck in the screaming crowd
where emaciated donkeys went at it
with that long bloody tube, which still scares me.

Oh, and my mother!—

her nightgown smelled like vinegar,
hem frayed, vibrant as a lemon.
My mother! She'd climb into bed
with a noise like a waterfall,
my mother—her full rich thighs—
whose ripe buttocks pinched the linen sheet between them
and drove me wild—should I be saying this?

A cruder calmer shame:
my sister, home from school, peeling her ice-wet bloomers down
so I could watch a delicate thread of urine
squirt from her tight pink lips!

Forgive me!

Evenings sometimes I saw my father, cursing,
playing cards with his neighbor—me they pushed away—things
seen . . .a father's scary . . . kids imagine things!
His knee, rubbing against a leg of the table,
his pants, his fly I wanted to unbutton—stop me!—
to hold the thick moist cock of this man
whose hairy hand rocked me!

And I won't talk about
the pot, the omelette pan, the handle, glimpsed in the attic,
almanacs streaked with blood, basket of lint,
the Bible, the maid fingering herself,
The Holy Virgin and the crucifix.

Oh, no one
was aroused so often, no one was so amazed!
Dear Lord, forgive me,
bathe me in Your grace, hear my confession,

let me speak to You as I would to a friend.
Puberty's never left me, and it grows, and the disgrace
of my tenaciously sensitive penis! Why,
why the slow heat at the base of my belly, why
raucous terrors burying my joy like black gravel
scattered by an anonymous hand?
That I exist astonishes me! What can I know?

Forgiven? O childhood! Nothing has changed.
I reach down: Lord, let's You and I jack off!

MAY BANNERS

In the shiny lime branches something is dying,
words celebrate, words thrash in currant branches
blood chortles in our veins, vines twist on themselves,
sky blessed us like an angel,
blueness and its blue wave commune,
I rush out into the street,
if one ray of sun stabs me I'll die on a hillock of moss,
patience and boredom are too simple,
fuck every one of my cares!
I want hysterical summer to strap me to its fateful chariot,
mostly because of you, Nature—less useless, less alone,
I'll die where shepherds die because the world is what it is,
I'm willing to be drained by the seasons,
Nature, I give in to you with all my hunger and thirst,
feed me if it pleases you, give me water to drink,
nothing deceives me,
my parents, the sun?—they make me giggle
but I don't want to mock anything—
cure my bad luck.

III

CHAIR: FRAGMENTS

Under raw walls beating emaciated dogs

Our frenzied hearts honest as bronze bells!

June 1871 massacred by a coal-black being
　　we Jean Baudry Jean Balouche having made our wishes
　　come true died in this ambiguous belfry dedicated
　　to our hatred of headmaster Desdouets!

His vest bobbled up and down he hiccupped as if
　　the rose he had swallowed got stuck—I watched it!

Only sixteen wavy long auburn hair they married her off

Now she's in love with her seventeen-year-old son

You want to ruin us tawny apostle you'd like to
　　scalp us—on my thighbone! but I have two twisted
　　tattooed thighbones dangerous as clubs

Because each day in school you sweat so heavily on your coat
　　collars you could fry an egg on those collars because you're a
　　fake like a dentist's white coat a hairless riding school horse
　　frothing at the mouth long in the tooth you want to decimate
　　my forty years in office!

Thighbone thighbone thighbone writhing for forty years
　　on the edge of my cherished walnut chair the pressure of the
　　wood has branded my ass

Handle yourselves watch me watch you play with yourselves
　　fondling that sloppy organ I'll touch it forever with my
　　thighbone forty years wedded to the edge of my chair

Grocer enter your shop when the moon is trapped in its blue
     windows seize tins of chicory right in front of us sprinkle it

Oh these eternal sketches!

And the poet plastered on wine bangs his fist on the universe

Who occupies this chair this throne Henry V Tropmann
     who murdered the Klinks for their money?

This seat so poorly shaped it ties knots in my guts

There's a hole with splintery edges cut in it the chef sits on it
     snoring like a bassoon

It's raining softly on the town

Take care of it O my absent life artery exploding in a beggar's head
     don't let it go

Moonlight washes the church clock striking twelve

"My hands are dying" wept Regina

What notes from what bronze bell hearts dogs bleating under the
     shadow-haunted walls?

LICE KILLERS

The child's head swarming with red sores
implores white mystifying dreams
his two amiable adolescent sisters
thin-fingered silvery-nailed
stand near his bed
then sit their brother by an open window
air moist as a cloud honeysuckle twisted on the wall
their cautious conscious magical fingers slide
in and out of his dense dewy hair
he hears their nervous breathing
laced with the rose-honey of plants
interrupted off and on
by the hiss of spittle caught on a lip
or the wish for kisses
hears their swarthy eyelashes beating the aromatic silence
fingers electric sweet swimming his indolence
the deaths of the lice—so tiny!—crackle under their queenly nails
then the good red wine of sloth rises through every pore
a sigh like a glass harmonica echoes in his delirium
under their slow caresses the urge to cry surges up and dies
    incessantly

PARISIAN ORGY

Fucking cowards, She's right outside—here is the holy city, enthroned in the West! pile out onto the station platforms, sunlight has scoured the boulevards the treacherous lower classes jammed one night,

Follow me, we'll stave off future fires, here are the quays, here the boulevards, the houses hurled against pale radiant blue studded one night with the star-like spark showers of grenades!

Hide the corpses of palaces with forests of planks, terrified daylight bleaches your faces, watch the troop of red-headed hip-wrigglers, go crazy, crack jokes, dance till your faces are drained!

Mob of bitches in heat, gorge on poultices, the wail from the bank vaults swollen with gold beckons you—plunder, eat, describe the night of joy and fathomless twitchings descending on the street, O you ravaged drunks,

Drink—when dawn comes to ransack every rustling luxury around you, dumb and frozen won't you drool into your glasses your eyes lost in silver distances?

Drink to the Queen whose buttocks cascade in sloppy folds, listen to the mechanics of stupid weepy hiccups, listen to the panting idiots, old people, nonentities, lackeys leap through the night that's a wall of flame!

Hearts constructed of shit, repulsive smelly mouths work harder, more wine for these shameful torpors slumped over tables. . . . Disgrace melts your bellies, Conquerors!

Open your nostrils to these sublime nauseas, sniff their rare perfume, steep the tendons of your necks in strong poisons, I, the poet say to

you, laying my crossed hands on the napes of your childish necks—
O cowards, be as insane as you really are!

Because you rummage the guts of the Female you're afraid she'll
thrash like a bucket of hungry snakes, cry out, stifle your infamous
sitting on her breasts with so much pressure it could kill her.

Syphilitics, kings, puppets, psychotics, ventriloquists how can you
mean anything to that whore Paris, how can your souls, bodies, poi-
sons, rags touch her? She'll crush you, diseased harmless snarlers!

And when you grovel on your bellies, whimpering, ribs kicked in,
begging for your money back, in a trance, tits bulging with battle the
red prostitute will shake her iron fists utterly disdainful, cut off from
your sleeping minds!

Paris, when your feet spun furiously in anger, riddled with knife
wounds, when you lay helpless your eyes clear still reflecting a shred
of the goodness of tawny spring,

Mutilated city, comatose city, your face and both breasts pointing
towards the Future whose trillion gates swing open to your ashen
skin, city the dark Past may bless,

Body galvanized back to life only to be tortured, you swallow intol-
erable life again, you feel white worms gush back into your veins and
ice-cold fingers prowl your pure love!

But it doesn't faze you, the worms can't strangle your breath of
Progress any more than the Styx could blind the Caryatides' eyes
whose stone sills dripped with tears of sidereal gold.

Horrible to see you smothered again like this though no city ever
became a more putrid ulcer on the face of green Nature, I, the Poet,
say to you "Your beauty is miraculous!"

Your fate sealed in perfect poetry by the hurricane that ripped you to pieces, massive strength helps you, your labors boil over, I can hear the death rattles—City elected by fate, treasure those who stride

The raving trumpet, the Poet will gather up each sob of each criminal, hate of the galley-slaves, screams clawing off the lips of the damned, and his resurrecting love will plague all women, his stanzas

Pounce on the villains that caused this—every table, chair, window, steeple, church wall, flower, wine glass brought back to life, Society exists again, and the orgies shed dry tears in the dank crumbling

Brothels, on walls muralled with blood sinister gaslight shadows flicker and grieve reaching up to the thin blue skies, every brick and treetrunk burns with a new reality, everything rebuilt, nothing left but a memory.

HER HANDS

Jeanne-Marie has powerful hands rich brown hands tanned by
summer hands pale as the hands of corpses

where did their dusky cream-colored hue come from—sailing on
lakes of sexual pleasure dipped into moons in serene ponds

sunk on beguiling knees have they torn down prehistoric skies rolled
cigars calmly slaved in the diamond markets

thrown gold roses at the flaming feet of Madonnas? The black blood
of belladonnas sleeps and shines in their palms

hands that drive the diptera buzzing with auroral blue toward the
nectar hands that dole out doses of poison

what dream changes them to iron whipping the top of hands mani-
acal vision of Asias Zions Khenghavaras?

these hands have never sold oranges got sunburnt at the gods' feet
washed the diapers of heavy eyeless babies

not hands of a whore or working women's whose round drenched
foreheads baked by the sun high on the scent of tar in woods reek-
ing of factories mirror the world's grief

predictable as machines tougher than oxen these hands bend
backbones refuse to harm you

no chill of fear can withstand these blast furnaces their flesh howls
battlesongs sacrificial hymns thus we eat the enemy's gunfire

such hands could squash your neck pulverize your hands O evil
noble women notorious hands loaded with white and vermillion

glimpsing the splendor of these hands-of-love lambs turn their heads our mogul the sun places a ruby on each spicy finger

menacing dye of the common people stains them brown like the nipples of countesses every freedom fighter aches to kiss the backs of these hands

miraculous hands bleached by victorious sunlight 1871 Commune rebel hands on the bronze casings of machine-guns when Paris rose up fueled by compassion infinitely loyal to our cause!

sometimes O sanctified hands a chain of blinding links weeps on your wrist lips always drunk on confiscated wine quiver against your skin

and a sudden baffling force sizzles through our beings when those angelic hands try to make their sunburn fade by cutting themselves until they bleed

SLEEPER IN THE VALLEY

Green hollow where a stream chirps snatching silver shreds of itself in the grass sun flung from the proud mountain this narrow valley brimming with light

Young bare-headed pale soldier mouth open nape of his neck soaking in chilly blue cresses sleeps stretched on his bed of grass light raining down

His feet lie in the yellow flags he's asleep smiling the way a sick child might Nature cradle him warm him he's so cold even in the sun taking a nap

No scent of earth or pungent flowers can make his nostrils quiver his hands curled on his breast silent at peace two bright red holes in his right side

Nobody sees him nobody comes by to lean over his face and listen louder than this boy the miniscule voices of the grass seem to be trying to wake him

BLACKCURRANT RIVER

Can't believe Blackcurrant River dawdles through unmapped
valleys; hundreds of raucous crows follow it,
theirs is the true merciful voice of angels—acres of fir trees
loom like a tidal wave when the winds cut across.

Every inch of reality flows with the atrocious mysteries
of primeval landscapes, of fortresses overrun by tourists, large
estates—listen, on these banks you'll hear the dead passions
of dissolute knights: Oh but the wind is wholesome!

Traveler, peer through these clerestories, they'll make you braver
on your sleepless road. Soldiers of branches and leaves sent by God,
adorable joyous crows, assail the cunning peasant, drive him
out of here, this thief who clinks glasses with his old elbow stump!

FAUN'S HEAD

A kiss sleeps in the ambiguous green casket of foliage
flecked with gold, foliage studded with flowers,
bursts through the tapestry of lush cold leaves

A startled faun bites the dark red flowers with white teeth
two eyes peek through, his bloodied mouth
laughs under the branches

And when he leaps away like a squirrel his laugh
still vibrates on every leaf, a bullfinch panics the Gold Kiss
of the Wood contracting into itself again before it yields

To the faun's mouth wounded with mellow wine
kiss of reality kiss of the myth of love
O briefly visible presence nowhere again

LILIES

Arc of the sea-saw, strict, invisible, O you Lilies, silver enemas, enemies of work, enemies of famine—dawn floods your lucent tissues with purifying love, healing each wound, a nameless sacred sweetness butters your stamens!

CUPBOARD

A large carved cupboard of white oak
emanates that relaxed gentle air
old people have; open, its kindly
shadows give off fragrances like fine

wine, it overflows with a jumble
of quaint frayed things: sweet
yellowed linen, torn women's clothes,
faded laces, grandmothers' shawls

embroidered with griffins, children's shirts;
there must be lockets buried somewhere,
locks of white or blond hair, portraits
and dried flowers whose odors mingle

with the smell of apples and pears. O old-fashioned
cupboard, what stories you must know, it's obvious
you'd love to tell them each time your wide doors
slowly open and you clear your throat

PAROXYSMS OF CAESARS

He bites a cigar strolling the flowery lawns
black coat pants hat, wreathed in tatters of smoke,

face paler than the smoke, remembering the Tuileries
drenched in flowers. Now and then his dull eyes gleam

through his grief, drunk on his twenty-year orgy
when he lived by this sentence: "I'll blow out Liberty

as if it were a birthday candle—poof—like that!"
But Liberty's here again; sick, in prison,

it broke his back—ah, what vindictive name wets
his quivering lips, what unshakable remorse

eats out his guts? We'll never know, Napoleon IIIs
eyes are dead. Maybe he thinks of his old bespectacled

accomplice Emile Ollivier who didn't oppose
his emperor's declaration of war in 1870,

maybe he's back on his St. Cloud estate evenings
head hidden by a transfiguring shroud of blue smoke.

OPHELIA

Ophelia floats hallucinated lily asleep
adrift in her long veils
stars doze on the still red water
a death-knell echoes from distant woods

Ophelia's been dead more than a thousand years
white ghost pulled down the long river
her insanity reciting its ballad softly
for more than a thousand years

Wind loosens her elegant undulant veils
unravels twines them into a wreath
willows shiver on her shoulders
rushes quiet her spacious dreamy brow

The ruffled petals of water-lilies—
because of you sometimes a bird wakes from a slumbering alder
rustle of tiny wings leaving a nest
baffling hymn sung by the golden stars

Delicate as snow exquisite wan Ophelia!
It's true you died stolen by a river
ruthless Norwegian winds spilled in from the treacherous
mountains whispering bitter freedom to you

A breath twisted your thick tresses
filled your mind with rumors nobody understood
it was your heart hearing Nature's deceitful song
trees groaning nights like children in tears

It was the howling mania of brutal seas
that split your young vulnerable heart
it was the white-skinned nobleman one April dawn
the dumb madman who sat on your knees

Heaven exists! Love exists! Freedom exists!
that was your dream pathetic girl
the passion of his love kept you alive
speechless visions infinity's terror blinded your blue eyes!

This poet says you seek under starlight
flowers you picked and plaited into a gown
he sees you in your swaying veils eyes closed forever
an immense fragrant lily mirrored in the water

THIRST: FRAGMENTS

Wine waits at the beach for us millions of blue
waves hurtle from the mountain tops
good pilgrims we'll sip cloudy green absinthe
no more of these landscapes we'll get drunk friends
I'd rather rot under shit in a pond
like scum near floating driftwood no more
of those pure liquids water-lily cups
mouthless intimate hydra that eats all

Maybe long evenings await me I'll drink
in peace in a quiet town die happily
patient as I am if my pain leaves
if I ever have any gold should I
go North or stake out the Country of Vines
so shameful to dream dreaming's pure loss I'm
the old explorer once more so the green inn
won't open its warm doors to me again

Pigeons flicker in the shady meadow
the game of speed that sees and lives in the night
striped water-animals beasts in chains
the last butterflies! all thirsty
like me self-portraits roses graveyards light
emptied of everything except gray stone let me
dissolve where the rootless cloud dissolves let
me die in those damp waking violets every-

where among trees grass praying in deep woods

SQUATTING

It's like this: whenever his belly aches Brother Milotus glances at the skylight, sun blasts through it bright as a polished copper pot, blinds him, gives him a headache, he yawns and squirms and rubs his priestly tummy under the sheets

then flaps like a dying fish, gets up, gropes for the washbasin scared shitless he's swallowed his teeth; his gaping flannel nightshirt has to be buttoned before he can walk—still searching for his teeth, his fat gut drags him down

then shivers, squats, toes tucked under his feet; cracker-yellow sunlight smears the windowpanes papered at the top, frescoes the old man's shoulders, face and breast; his nose glows like a fleshy polyp lacquered red, he lifts his head sniffing the light

then stews by the fire, drooling onto his gut; his thighs slip, relax and settle, his pipe goes out, his underwear nearly catches fire, what once was a gorgeous warbler gurgles and squeaks inside this ambassador of God, his paunch squashy as a heap of tripe

chairs with their legs pulled off or splintered, cabinets punched in, wineglasses knocked to the floor, this grimy anarchic wreckage bulges everywhere—and then you see it: unbelievable turds like floppy toads scattered in corners, sideboards collapsed starving for love and sleep

the narrow room is stifling, this bum of a holy man's brain's crammed with scrap metal, spongy wood, wire, any kind of junk, he thinks he hears the roots of his hair sneak up through his sweaty scalp, he belches, hiccups importantly, shocks the weak stool he straddles then night: the moon's azure frosting the walls, dribbling on his bare ass, kindles a rich black phosphorescent shadow across a pink snowdrift pinker than blushing summer roses—what a peculiar nose tinted by the moon tracks Venus's journey all night long!

THE JUST MAN*

Get him away from me the one whose throat
flaunts the necktie of shame always aware
of my boredom like the shriek of sugar on a bad tooth
like the bitch attacked by horny males
that lick her torn flank guts trickling from it
The Just Man sat up straight on his firm ass
a single ray of light gilded his shoulder
I sweated—"Meteors flaming white stars
humming swarms of asteroids"—you want
to see them? he stood still bluish terror of lawns
after sundown I leapt up in revolt
O heart fallen among the chalices
majesties virtues love blindness
you are the eye of god your tenderness
serenity reason blow like whales at night
they stone you piss funeral words on ugly
broken doorknobs you're a coward eye of God
though the icy soles of the divine feet
smashed my neck you coward! head
seething with gnats Socrates Jesus
holy and just—disgusting! kneel to the supreme
Cursed One roaming bloodstained nights—This
is what I cried on earth while the tranquil white
night drenched the skies during my fever I lifted
my head the phantom had run off stealing my tongue's
vengeful irony O night winds soothe
the Cursed One speak to him while silently
under pale blue pillars past comets through interstices
of the universe an infinite rumble

without disasters Order The Eternal
Watchman rows across the luminous heavens
letting shooting stars spill from his flaming dragnet!

(July 1871)

*I have leaned heavily on Oliver Bernard's fine prose translation in *Arthur Rimbaud, Collected Poems* (Penguin Classics), and used some of his language *verbatim* in this pastiche of the poem.

FEASTS OF HUNGER

Anne, Anne, my hunger, ride your donkey into the sky,
if I like anything it's stones, dirt, oh my hunger,
eat rock air iron coal, feed on the meadow of sounds,
drag your muzzle in it, suck out the gaudy poison of convolvuli,
gnaw the stones a poor man sledgehammers into powder,
old church masonry, boulders, children floods have fucked
into existence, loaves rotting in gray valleys! Hunger,
it's bits of black air, the sea-blue trumpeter, my guts
that crucify me, it's unhappiness—listen to the curled shoot
of the pea wail near the acacias in April; in a crystal haze
old saints' heads float across like clouds . . . so far
from the tan cliffs rising in stacks, from green copper roofs,
these million-year-old brothers desperate for the potion
that slyly makes their pricks hard . . . Anne, Anne, flee
on your donkey, leaves have appeared on earth
for the first time and the sleepy flesh of fruit, the fox yelps
under leaves spitting out a woodcock's brightest feathers—
like him I devour myself—the hedge spider nibbles only violets,
salads and fruit can't wait to be picked, give me sleep, let me
simmer on Solomon's altar, let the scum drip down over
the rust of . . . neither the gold of haloes or stars, mist
exhaled by the night, and yet in this insane thin fog
every country remains—Sicily, Germany—I shit on all of it!
Seasons, steeples, is one human soul blameless?
Someone bangs a shovel against a wall, I kneel
in a furrow and pick Venus's Mirror and pluck up worms,
I tracked down the magic secrets of bliss, no one can escape it!
I hope it lasts forever, it overwhelms me, I need
nothing, it dissipates every effort. Do my words cure you?
They evaporate, O seasons, steeples, even the air
hears me and is happy.

LAST LINES: MEMORY: GOD

I

firm sad whiteness of women's bodies attacking the sun, stinging like a child's tears, clear water, silk lily-white banners massed beneath walls a girl defends, angels leaping—no—a gold current snaking this way and that flails its arms like a tired illusion, cool absolutely cool, hammered out of green, the female weed is sinking, Heaven's cobalt for a roof, shadows of the hill, archways for curtains

II

oh surface scattering its lucid bubbles, the water's a frail gilt bottomless coverlet for all the made beds, it's as if wild birds thrash out of little girls' grass-green hazy dresses masquerading as willows, eyelid warm yellow eyelid purer than a gold coin, marsh marigold, faith of the conjugal spouse, exactly at noon, coin that envies the rose-red sacred Sphere fainting with heat

III

Mrs. Nobody stands too straight in the nearby meadow where the pallid threads of the spider's task snow down, parasol twirled in her fingers, crushing the cow-parsley, so proud of her life, children reading in the lush rank air their red morocco book! Like thousands of chalk-white angels breaking up on the highway, He tunnels through the mountains! too bad our God's no longer God, and she, chilly as a thin shadow, runs after the man chasing after—God, or what?

IV

everywhere nostalgia for the burly young arms of virgin green! his
hymn to God proves He is mortal, outcry, elegy of the unknown
memory, ingot of April moons sunk in the heart of the deified bed,
joy of defunct shipyards, what August twilight prey thrilled these cor-
ruptions?—she weeps now bereft under the parapets, poplars' breath
swims over us, all there is for a breeze, then the barrier of opaque
gray water starting from nowhere, an old man, dredging for some
great treasure, toils furiously in his motionless boat

V

eye of mournful water, plaything I can't reach, O vessel of glacial
immobility, O too short arms! either this flower or that one over
there but not the yellow beauty importuning me here, not the
darling periwinkle either, the one I love so much drowned in the
ashen water—oh God, pollen from the willows a sudden wing shakes
down, reed roses long since eaten away, my boat still safe its anchor
chain a taut arterial line pulled straight to the bottom of this finite
eye of water, its anchor clutching slime

VI

why should we care about it, heart, why study the sheets of blood,
red-hot coals, lynchings by the thousands, the drawn-out wails of
rage under the eyes of a missing God—not missing, non-existent—
grieving in every hell dismantling every fabricated order, the North
wind churning across the wreckage—is it all merely vengeance? No,
nothing, but Yes, we need we beg for industrialists princes senates
colleges, all of you—die! power justice history—go down! we
deserve nothingness, it's on its way, I can see the invisible troops,
blood blood the putrid flame of money ending it, squirm in your

own greedy wound, end every empire regiment colony, and God
who never was

VII

who will stoke the dizzying homicidal flames but us and our
brothers, it's our turn idealistic friends, revel in it, scorch your faces,
no more work, waves higher than steeples, rachitic lightning—
Europe Asia America vanish, each place that exists sucked into bits by
our vindictive tornado, cities countrysides, we'll be crushed, volca-
noes will shear off our heads, the ocean fall in love or dry up—dear
friends, my heart, nothing can stop it—brothers, sunburnt strangers,
we begin, I feel it, follow me, fate of evil I can't stop shivering as if
I'm the wind itself hopelessly estranged from all facts—dear earth,
old earth, I can feel you melt over me, earth, hearth fire, more and
more yours, even without the word God I'm one with you

it's nothing   *I am here*   *I'm still here*

RIMBAUD: IV

THE IMPOSSIBLE
(for Lou Asekoff)

Rain, snow, icestorms, peaceful sunny days, I was riveted to life, a beggar cruising the endless road. Oblivious, stupid, proud, preternaturally calm, who needed friends or country?

O my ecstatic childhood, I was right to hate what I hated. Listen: in Hell we don't give even the dying a penny, but we're civil. We see the world correctly. We're not salesmen. Nothing hurts us, not even the surly, confident ones, the false elect, who humiliate us, refuse to bless us.

Western swamps, you've sponged up all the light! My soul won't stop grieving. I'd have to strangle myself to end these same arias honestly.

When I confronted the King of Hell, I said: Fuck martyrdom, fuck the sublime health of art, the seriousness of inventors, the fervor of businessmen and thieves. The East is a dream of never waking up. I wasn't pondering my escape from contemporary anguish. I wasn't exploring the spooky Koran. Ever since Science took over, Man hides from himself. We cultivate fog, eat fever with our watery carrots and broccoli. We get drunk, smoke, sacrifice ourselves. Infinitely distant from the root, we exterminate ourselves with our own poisons.

Rabbis and priests, this is not Eden. Time doesn't exist. The world has no age. Formulate your own East, older than the stars. Don't give in. You're free to live beyond suicidal schemes of salvation. Science is much too slow for men like us. Cherished Western citizens, wake up. Your souls are asleep. You're still addicted to the human. Truth's everywhere, as close as our own hands. Weeping angels hover close to us. Soul, soul, this radiant instant—sinister turning of ten windmills by the edge of a bare field in a black and hungry year—crucifies us.

LIGHTNING

Human work—eyes, hands, fingers, toes, groins squeezed against metal! Necessity, grenade after silent grenade, explodes in distant corners of my abyss, whenever it wants to.

Work is much too slow. What can I do? Turn prayer into a wild horse! Let light thunder! I see it, it's so simple, so clear—hotter than a furnace door. You won't need me when you see it too.

Pity me—my life is like a cheap torn coat. Reality cries fuck and eat everything, desecrate the world's masks: politician, beggar, poet, sleazy administrator . . . priest! When I was in the hospital—what was it?—wisps of the stink millions of people left behind in confession boxes, a kind of acrid, sacred residue in homage to our tragedy, suffocated me, exposed the half-baked education I got as a child. So what? I can reach twenty, if you can.

Listen, you bastards—I refuse to die. Work is trivial, my pride won't tolerate its chain of empty minutes.

Priceless fragile soul, are we cut off from eternity forever? Would that teach us to be free?

Oh now I can hear Mankind lifting its hopeful voice: "Vanity doesn't exist! Science is salvation! Move your asses!" while the corpses of parasites and convicts freeze the hearts of humble men like us. Beyond night itself, beyond even the most remote planetary edge of the future, God waits to redeem us, and we can't shun that fate.

HAPPINESS

Each of us is doomed to be happy, forced to live many lives. Each of us will be crushed on the anvil of terror, reborn by awe. Action isn't life, it spoils God's power, it drains the last prayers from our throats. The soul's theater is invisible—sight, hearing, taste, smell, senses without organs.

Listen: each of us lives many lives—plumbers, angels, athletes, electricians, gods. Once I was a pig. I champion all axioms of madness. I lived them all, I know the system.

Terror gnaws my mind. The same dream drags me back into it, destroys the real world, calls me to inhabit it permanently. I'm ready to die, ready to be wind, darkness, ghosts.

God's final curse is a live coal broiling my tongue. Islands and blue sea, I dream you'll wash away this disease of unspecified truths, I see the cross loom like redemption. The rainbow led me here, where remorse swims like a tapeworm dragging itself out past my lips. My life is immense, I won't dedicate myself to muscle and rhyme.

Deadly sweet tooth of bliss, solo—in the gloomiest cities, at dawn, you warn me. I hear you first in the gossip of the men who raped my mouth and ass. Then in windswept leaves. Two truths. One truth. That's the final terror we all have to accept—not one or the other, but both, like a friend's face whose torn-out eyes still recognize you.

WORDS

The tiny bud scared me. Vicious landscape. I did everything to escape it. I told people I could visit them inside me, mocked the current darlings of poetry. Their courteous bows to the smug audience of approval made me puke.

Porno magazines, rotting Victorian travel books, medieval passion plays, junked movie sets, refrains from old songs, languages I couldn't read, musty albums packed with snapshots of the family desperately trying to smile—through all of it I saw that hard young body begging to be loved.

I even invented a religion without icons or rites. I wrote a brief manual of prayers and regulations, I established walking and sleeping as the two basic forms of sacrifice. I described God: obese, lazy, dressed like a stockbroker in His pink shirt and chalk-striped flannel suit, puffing on a cigar.

I invented vowel colors, reshaped the cadence of consonants, consigned each syllable to a branch on the elm outside my house. I deleted the senses from poetry until all I could hear was a faint abstract whisper like the breathing of a horse thirty feet away. English! English! My precise identity babbled its proofs in dreams.

Nothing worked. I wrote silence. I wrote night. On scraps of wrapping paper, I scratched down hopeless love. I paced my crummy room like a squirrel—significant, hyper-acute, pathologically quick—

but she would not be erased, a thousand years younger by then, spread-eagle across my mind, inches from my face, the gash between her legs, its ethereal brown hair and wild node, a crown I licked all over until she came.

BLACKS

The blood of black Neanderthals heats my veins. Holy spirit, you're near. Why doesn't Christ help me? The Gospel's garbage on the street in front of a whorehouse.

I wait for God like a man watching all his money in stocks plummet. Cell by cell, I'm doomed, I'll never rise above these roots.

I stand on a western beach. Let houselights, streetlights flare when evening comes. My days on earth are finished. West, your salt sea air sears my lungs, islands and weird empires bake my skin. I want to bathe in those waters, trample grass, hunt, smoke, get drunk on booze as strong as boiling metal, crouched like my ancestors at the fringes of campfires.

When I come home my arms will be iron, skin like a starless night, eyes like a tiger's. Pouches of gold will dangle from my waist, I'll be idle, brutal. People will fear me. Politics will save me. I'll lose myself in politics. Women will offer me their naked breasts and hot cunts.

I hate this country. I was born exiled. How else can I become God, how else can His mute invisible clarity occur? I'm going to drink this whole bottle, right now, sleep on the sand, dream a world-shaking theory I can't prove: The mystery of God is the mystery of one's own identity . . . etc.

IMAGE

Rimbaud, civilization handcuffs you. These aphoristic gunshots aren't poetry. You're so fucked-up no technique can shape your despair. I heard whoever I am speak, I followed you, repeated words, exchanged their meanings, hallucinated chemical shifts—a rose into a tree, a living room under a lake, long black roads jammed with carriages in the sky, a school of drummer boys conducted by an angel, babies' heads on old bodies—I alchemized my heart into a black stone. Music of words stripped of meaning, exposition to deify lyricism, formulas like "God is, by definition, without dimension . . ." became eschatological proofs. I prayed the melodrama of my lost faith would raze cities, bark not sing, reverse existence.

My personal chaos became a makeshift religion. I started that fad in society. I was the one! Sweet animals, caterpillars drugged by their innocent limbo, arrogant moles, smooth deep sleep of virgins! I wanted to be anyone but me—whoever that was. I wanted to be the one understandable word on a tablet in a cryptic tongue.

Finally I stared into the mirror until the boy in the glass and the boy outside were one, then smeared the word GOD on it with a shitty forefinger.

GOD

I'm not bored. No rage, faggotry, madness—I'm relaxed now. Clear your minds, consider my innocence. I'm not asking for pity. I don't want to marry Christ's daughter. Listen: I'm not limited by my rational mind. I told God I want death. That's the one freedom. These days I'm concentrating only on what's essential. No frivolous tidbits, no devotion, no need of divine love. No sadness over the age of my sensitive heart. Each of us has reason, scorn, gratitude. Let me take my place on top of the angelic ladder of common sense.

Familial happiness? It's not for me. I'm too dissolute, too weak. Life thrives through toil—numb platitude! My life isn't heavy enough, it flies and floats high above action, that precious focus of the world.

God, give me celestial airy calm, reverence, sainthood, change me into an angel whose work sings God instantly into men's flesh, blood, marrow. Nobody wants that anymore. What a perpetual farce. What a naïve idiot I am. I'm practically an old maid. I don't have the balls to love death,

obsessed with that transcendentent image of mine, oh, that sick psalm—one lone fly drunk in a hotel toilet, crazy with excrement, cooked by a random shaft of sunlight!

PAIN

The rich can't sleep. Wealth should be everyone's. All the rich know is lineages, but I've had to transcend my own suicidal habits, my own muzzled gift for oblivion. Now I'm good. Nothing to repent. But the clock still strikes the hour of absolute pain. Will I end up like a child, in Paradise, without sorrow?

Divine love's the only key to knowledge. Nature's a display of pure goodness. I'm through with demons.

The rational song of angels teaches salvation: Divine Love. I'll die of worship, of loving the razed earth—both! I condemn anyone my departure would destroy. Save my friends, save the shipwrecked passengers!

This ground under my feet is good. Sane at last, I'll bless life, love my brothers. No more childish promises. No hope of escaping old age and death. My strength is God. Praise God! His omnipotent abstract transparent hands soothe my face.

No early death for me—sons of good families, coffins glistening with crystal tears. I've been rescued by the white man, converted, baptized, dressed in work clothes, chained to a job. What a relief! Christianity's blade, stuck straight through my heart.

SUBLIMITY

Even as a child the incurable convict gorged me with awe, all those doors closing behind him, that chorus of iron. Steel skies, fields bursting with wild asters—I knew they were his idea of himself, his raw, particular fate. He alone witnessed his own glory. Reasonable mind, tenacious as a saint, more practical than a tourist, a seeker everywhere, nothing could tear his image out of my head.

Winter nights on an empty road, naked, without bread, a voice froze my heart: "Weak or strong, it's you: pointlessly walking, go in anywhere, say anything to anyone, they won't kill you, you're already a corpse. That's your strength."

Suddenly the black and red mud of cities was a mirror, a lamp carried back and forth in a locked room, winking under the door, a gold shield in a forest. Good luck, I yelled. A sea of smoke and flames, all the wealth in the world, flashed like a billion thunderbolts, looted the sky!

A screaming mob caught me. Blindfolded, propped up in front of a firing squad, I wept out of pity for the evil they could not grasp, and forgave them. "Priests, professors, misers, merchants, generals, my white masters, I'm from a race that sings under torture. A brute, a black beast whose eyes can't see your courteous light. I can't be saved. Let the law kill me. I have no morality, this is a mistake!"

Do I know nature yet, do I know myself? Not one more syllable. I'm digging a grave in my belly for the dead. Howls, drumming, delirious savage dances.

HANDS

Beggars are too honest, they disgust me. Blue-white my eyes, skull cramped as a broom closet. I'm like the Gauls, I don't butter my hair. With the splendid disdain of kings, I love all the vices.

Bosses and workers, slaves, the hand that writes with the pen guides the plough. History is hands! Will I never possess my hands, be cared for by invisible gods, fed by the sky, entertained by water? Devious tongue. I'm lazier than a toad. Feeble, Christian notes, lovesong, what was I in the last century?

You geniuses at profit and loss, what is the body? Do you recognize your body? Progress is a great god with a mouth and no asshole. The cosmos is a mechanical toy. Chemistry in a teaspoon. The world moves forward, an army without shoes.

The revelation of fate in numbers is clear. I can't explain what I mean. I'm not a ditchdigger, I don't fix wagons or doors. Driven toward the Soul, like hungry cattle, I hear sounds without reference to things outside themselves—the poor a clashing Hell of symbols. Your demolished silence, a king with no mouth.

SEEDS

Inside this wailing skin, I'm still alive. Shirt of flame, remember Paradise! Purged of all human hope, like a huge cat, I mutilated joy's face, chewed on my executioners' wings. Disaster was my God, I groveled in mud, dried myself off in the breezes of crime. I acted crazier than myself. Spring's psychotic laughter crushed my heart.

I dined at the sacred feast that gave me back my appetite. Infant soul, I knew the tiniest gesture of your finger, lip or eyelid was a rite of mercy, a suicidal plea.

NOSTALGIA

Why look back at the old roads again? Drugs and buggery flour-
ished. My grief took root. Why inspect each vice that started when
thought dawned? It hurts the sky, drags me into the stone future.

This is the last innocence, the last introverted peek into the reamed-
out precincts of Hell, the last choral swoon. It's over—betrayals,
disgusts, my effigies of a metaphysical unknown.

Who wants to hire me? What beast should I adore? What face of the
divine defile? Whose hearts should I break? What lies should I
defend? What blood should I wade through?

Avoid the police. Live poor. With a withered fist lift the coffin lids,
sit until you evaporate. *Mon ami*, terror isn't French.

I'm so alone nothing about me rises above the paltry earth.

My punishment? To take one step after another, lungs frozen, head a
blast furnace, my daylight eyes drenched with night.

Time duplicates us after death. Where? Will we really be the same?

Shoot me in the face or I'll jam this pistol into my raving mouth,
jump under those wheels. . . . Believe me, I welcome it.

IMPASSE METANOIA

Fire in my guts, dose of holy poison crippling me, I'm a live corpse almost reborn, but I slipped away. Happy, good, I'm ready for salvation, and yet Hell won't tolerate my song of insolent hope.

Life grinds us into ash. My parents baptized me, that watery bliss enslaved me, slaughtered me with ardor.

Hell, bless me! Only fresh crime could plunge me into nothingness. Give me Justice, Her scales emptied of the past.

Childhood comes back: grass, rain, the lake over stones, moonlight oozing through the roof of the belfry when the bell struck midnight. Fatal ignorance, nursery rhymes, Mary, Virgin Mary, you're a lie! Don't touch me. I smell like roasted skin.

This is truth— There's no history. Wealthier than a king, I decode secret wisdoms, postulate the immortality of tables and chairs.

Life's clock stopped hours ago. Theology is somewhere else. Straddling a green wave, Jesus walks on purple thistles, Jesus walks on the stormiest water. This ecstatic sleep of mine unveils the mysteries.

Have faith, follow me, crippled, exhausted laborers, fragile children— astonished human heart!

Hell, I'm sold on your glory, your worms and pitchforks, holocaust of lust— I've decided to be reborn and study every maimed piece of myself, kissed by Mother Earth. God, hide me, hold me; these words, sniffing the ground, are starved dogs pocked with sores.

I'm hidden, and absolutely clear.

Smear dress shop mirrors with wet dirt, choke lovers in bed with powdered rubies—change me. I live and live and live.

ANGEL

Lost. Drunk. Covered with shit. But listen. Forgive me. Down here. Friends. No friends. Raped by ghosts. Insane. Damned and dead. Grieving, terrified.

Testicles. Breasts. No city. I follow her. No choice. Punished, but I follow. Not a woman or man.

Reinvent love, whippings, blood, grovelings, that voice, like death itself, a little girl, singing, trapped in wordless pain.

No mind. A sleeping body. Watched. Outside, thinking. Dreams? Dangers? The key? Slaves of compassion, despair, we protected each other. We knew the world was here.

Angel in her soul. Sorrow. Two children locked in a Paradise of sorrow.

Sick with the terror of leaving, can anyone hear God? Shame of the sleepwalker.

I know: some day at the same moment we'll both disappear.

DAWN

I was young. A hero. They wrote my story in gold, my frantic tale of Hell. Real Hell. White-hot doors that open. Christ's hands and feet.

Eyes fixed on the silver star, my pain melted my eyes. I was the first one to sing the song of people under a fair sky.

Autumn. Infinite sun. Beyond the changing seasons, our tiny boat, fire, mud, wet bread. Love's mind nailed to a cross, love's actual gazes and touches.

Heart riddled with worms, cold earth, identify these strangers. Am I dead?

At times I see endless beaches of white nations, cured by raptures of joy. I lead festivals, victories, tragedies. I invent new flowers, new stars, new flesh, new speech.

Every pore of my feet kisses the ground. One task: to love reality like a peasant.

Am I wrong? Are death and charity twin sisters?

Forgive my lies.

No hands, no help.

Everything's clear! Don't move. Dried blood smokes on my face.

BEAUTY

Last night, I sat Beauty on my knees, kissed her, sniffed her dog's breath, cursed Justice, thrashed Hope out of my brain, gave up Religion, despised anything I could name, butchered Joy. I saw my rose of tenderness shriveled by fear, saw myself as a child when all hearts opened, all wines flowed, and I wanted to die.

But, in a great dream, I thought: Find the key to your life. And it appeared: Charity.

I shook black from the blackish night sky. I became a spark of raw golden light, a clown, a blank-faced clown, so carefree all I did was smile. My mind was like the sky on one of those mild bright late April days you wish would last forever. Not one cloud floated by. Consciousness was outside me, asking, "What are you going through?"

Is the idea of God enough, can it console you?

AFTERWORD

I can't pretend I knew what I was doing when some illegitimate urge drew me back to Rimbaud's poetry. I do know I felt close again to his poems in traditional forms, written before *Les Illuminations* and *Une Saison en Enfer*. The mood of his puerile genius attracted me—arrogant, disdainful, renegade rage; disgust, helpless compassion, hopeless yearning; infinitely dissatisfied, tender, loving in anti-love, politically bitter, distrusting pretension. With little French, I submitted my gift for theft gratefully to several stray translations in verse—chiefly to Oliver Bernard's prose translations of the *Collected Poems*. The Louise Varese translation of *Une Saison* is behind "Rimbaud," section IV of this book.

I had no method for my blindly composed experiment. Most of Rimbaud's poems in meter and rhyme are here.[1] I distorted some of them into prose poems because I was impelled to make versions outside the forms of the originals. The order of the poems is not chronological. I wanted to begin with fairly strict sonnets, and wind up with prose poems. I have been caught by similar projects before because the English translations I read did not seem to achieve a thorough enough transformation of the originals into good English poems. Each time this has happened I have been forced to proceed any way I could, use whatever materials I could find, not sure I could rescue living elements of the original.

In the late stages of revision, especially, I concentrated on the poems as English poems only, free to consider *any* change that might improve them, whatever the original in prose translation said. I do not apologize for this thoroughly corrupt approach. I had no choice. Once the momentum of the process was underway, and might fulfill itself, I was hooked, no matter what the quality of the results would be.

Rimbaud's pragmatic romanticism, his deliberate "emotional

derangement,"[2] his atheistic hunger for religious belief, his imma-
ture but compassionate hatred of political, emotional and moral
deceit and self-deceit continue to keep pace with humanity at odds
with itself. Bourgeois to the core, aware of the narcissistic mask of a
lie intrinsic to middle-class sympathy-without-participation for the
poor and disinherited, he was a deluded perfectionist—i.e. either a
person lives his or her values and beliefs or he must rebel against
himself and society as impossibly sick, dissonant identities. I hope I
have been able to intuit some of the tension of his naïve disillu-
sionment and protest, hope it will give readers examples of "what
they need in their situation."[3]

The combined assault that makes money, moral-political confusion
and existential despair a singular agony grew louder and louder in
Rimbaud's ears. He spent his late adolescence in an inspired
attempt to reintegrate his psyche, searching for a kind of personal-
social justice that would help him and others to survive the new
industrial world's bitter price—join it or be exiled within your own
society. One long evening in front of TV offers a vivid sketch of
what is out there now. Rimbaud pioneered the often vatic fusion of
descriptive imagery and intellect in poetry that expresses the begin-
nings of modern metaphysical distress. By overlapping categories of
experience and immersing them in his original acidic blend of
irony and innocence, he revised the basis of meaning in poetry,
hoping that the ethic of his esthetic would reform human greed
and ignorance. Poet of the impossible, he continues to stand for the
traumatized, self split by its desire to be a *pure* social being, an
incorruptible conscience that refuses to be both poet and business-
man at once. Language and action must be one was his Godless
religion, until he converted on his deathbed. Before his teens were
over he gave up language for action when he realized that a man—
first of all Arthur Rimbaud—could say anything and yet, comfort-
ably or not, live a life detached from his words, as if they were
merely beautiful insignificant abstractions. We all know that's what
most of us do—live as we live, unwilling to embody our beliefs.

Only the saint does one or the other; or becomes the koan that teaches him how to make word and deed one.

[1]Exceptions are "First Communion", "The Drunken Boat", "The Poet at Seven", "To the Poet on the Subject of Flowers", "Nina Replies, Sensation", "The Blacksmith", "The Orphans' New-Year's Gift", "Sun and Flesh", "The Famous Victory of Sarrebruck", "The Customs Men", "Parisian War Song", "Vowels", "The Old Guard and Brussels".

[2]T. S. Eliot, from a letter in which he refers to "my lifelong emotional derangement."

[3]Wallace Stevens, from *The Necessary Angel*.

103

ABOUT STEPHEN BERG

On the same day as this volume, Berg is publishing *The Elegy on Hats* with Sheep Meadow Press. Other books published by Stephen Berg include *Halo* (Sheep Meadow Press), *Clouded Sky: Poems by Miklos Radnoti* (Sheep Meadow Press), *The Daughters, Grief, With Akhmatova at the Black Gates, In It, The Steel Cricket,* and *Crow with No Mouth: Ikkyū.* He is the founder and coeditor of the *American Poetry Review,* and the recipient of Rockefeller, Guggenheim, NEA, Dietrich Foundation, and Pew fellowships.